Canyon de Chelly
National Park

Our Navajo elders called it Tseyi, referring to a "place within the rock." Their account of the place within the rock embraces the history of the human spirit, a place of refuge, and a source of strength, protection, and peace.

*T*he land itself inspires creativity and an intimate knowledge of plants and animals, giving our people a heritage we still value and practice today. As part of the family who call the canyon home, we welcome you to share in experiencing this "place within the rock."

Canyon de Chelly National Monument, located in northeastern Arizona, was set aside in 1931
to preserve the ruins of cliff dwellings built by prehistoric people between A.D. 350 and 1300.

Front cover: White House ruin, photo by Gail Bandini. Inside front cover: Navajo hogan, photo by Dick Dietrich. Page 1: Navajo pictographs of Spanish expedition, at Standing Cow Ruin, photo by Fred Hirschmann. Pages 2/3: Junction of Canyon de Chelly and Canyon del Muerto, photo by Tom Danielsen. Pages 4/5: Tseyi Overlook, photo by Tom Danielsen.

Edited by Cheri C. Madison.
Book design by K. C. DenDooven.

Fifth Printing, 2009 • New Version

in pictures CANYON DE CHELLY Nature's Continuing Story™
© 1999 KC PUBLICATIONS, INC.

"in pictures … Nature's Continuing Story™"; the Eagle / Flag icon on Front Cover are registered in the U.S. Patent and Trademark Office

LC 99-60056. ISBN 978-0-88714-145-4

in pictures

Canyon de Chelly

Nature's Continuing Story™

by Wilson Hunter, Jr.

WILSON HUNTER, JR., a Navajo, grew up near Tseyi Overlook. He is a member of the Coyote Pass Clan, and was born for the Bitter Water Clan. He began his park ranger career as a tour guide. Currently Chief of Interpretation at Canyon de Chelly National Monument, he is the recipient of the 1991 Freeman Tilden Award.

...the Story of Canyon de Chelly

GAIL BANDINI

*J*unction Ruin, *located at the intersection of the*
two main canyons. Isolated under an alcove, perhaps
one family occupied this site. Most of their daily activities
were conducted below, on the floor of the canyon.

Canyon de Chelly encompasses a rich cultural resource amid the beauty of the natural landscape. The history of the human spirit and its relationship with the environment here is both rich and complex. All the people who lived here and called the canyon "home," had a close relationship with the land and wove their strands within the canyon web of life. The canyon is unique today in that Navajo people continue to live within it. This pattern has its origin in antiquity. The opportunities to preserve and provide for the use of the resource are challenging for both the National Park Service and the Navajo. As the number of people using the canyon grows, littering, vandalism, and interference with the privacy of canyon residents all become concerns. The need for land management and an overall respect for its beauty and uniqueness are no different than those needed for the whole planet Earth. We all need to realize that humanity is tied to the land and is responsible for it.

"...the people *who lived here ...* wove *their* strands *within* the *canyon* web *of* life."

Sharing the trail with a herd of sheep is very common along the White House trail. Navajo sheepherders often take sheep up and down the trail during the summer.

"Home is where the heart is"—the phrase carries a feeling of security and well-being, a sense of place and belonging. Canyon de Chelly was home to Ancestral Puebloans who lived among the rock walls. Recently, it has been home to the Navajo people. During the summer, canyon residents are part of the scene, and their presence, their hogans and farms, reflects the continued significance of the canyon. It is important to remember as you visit the canyon, not only are you visiting a national monument, you are visiting a people's home.

Formation of the Canyon

Rain and water play an important part in the formation of the canyon, which is a major drainage system for high plateau and mountainous areas. The entire outflow from the canyon empties into the San Juan River. Located along the western edge of the Defiance Plateau, it is part of the Colorado Plateau. A major uplift in the Defiance Plateau began the formation of the canyon, and later water and wind played their role in sculpturing the fascinating formations we see today. The De Chelly sandstone formation deposited during the Permian Period is the most visible and recognizable formation in the canyon.

To the people who live here—and those who lived here in the past—there is no scientific meaning to the landscape. We have our creation stories of how the canyon was formed. The opportunity to live and survive with the land is considered a gift from our holy people. This land provides abundant food, water, and shelter. Homes were built from the resources available on the floor or blended into the rock alcoves. We understand the natural forces of nature and connect ties to create harmony with the land.

JAMES TALLON

JAMES TALLON

*R*ain, bringing moisture vital to the area, passes through in the distance east of White House ruin. Major perennial streams flowing from the nearby Chuska Mountains to the east cut the canyon terrain. Water flow is fairly constant during spring runoff and usually dry in the summer, except when seasonal thunderstorms appear daily during late summer.

*W*ater pockets reserve water on the rim of the canyon. Storms that bring water to the parched land are always welcome—however, the storms are short lived, lasting from about 20 minutes to 2 hours. The canyon people appreciate the opportunity to receive water for irrigation and fresh water for daily use, and to replenish the supply for their animals.

Millions of years ago windblown sand created huge dunes. Water saturation and pressure created the De Chelly sandstone. The erosion of the sandstone illustrates the different directions of the wind. To the Navajo this is evidence of what was created by the Wind People. The same concentric circles found on the eroding sandstone are found on the tips of our fingers. Also from the Wind People, we received our breath and thus can speak.

A good harvest of crops requires plenty of available water. Water is considered a valuable resource to the Southwest, and Canyon de Chelly is no exception. The canyon is located in a desert plateau surrounded by mountains, which results in generally low levels of precipitation. Although dry farming has been practiced for centuries in the Southwest, in recent years many residents of the canyon have chosen not to plant in the spring because of the lack of rainfall.

The beauty of the land and survival of life in a harsh environment are often evident along canyon walls—even in places where life seems almost impossible. Canyon people, from earliest times to the present, develop respect for the forces of nature and its influence on all living things. Harmony is needed for one's mental, physical, and emotional health. A loss of respect for natural forces will interrupt the natural cycles in the environment.

LARRY ULRICH

TOM DANIELSEN

The Early People

The Hopi, descendants of the prehistoric people, call the early people *Hisatsinom*, meaning "people of the long ago." Navajos called these early people *Anasazi*, a common word referring to all the ancient people whose dwellings and handmade tools and wares we find throughout the Southwest. The Navajos did not distinguish among the different Pueblo cultural groups as we do today. Archaeologists adopted the word Anasazi, and it is still commonly used for these people who migrated away from the canyon in the 1200s. The Pueblos today, however, object to their ancestors being called Anasazi, and would rather they be referred to as Ancestral Puebloans. Many of the ancient sites in Canyon de Chelly are still sacred and an important part of modern Pueblo culture. Traces of Hopi clan symbols are identified in early pictographs. These sites provide a bond for the Pueblos with their ancestors and have a place in their oral history which is passed down to the next generation.

LES MANEVITZ

GAIL BANDINI

Studies and scientific evidence show there has been continuous occupation around Canyon de Chelly from about A.D. 200 to at least A.D. 1300, but ample evidence from recent studies suggests that the area may have been occupied even earlier than A.D. 200. These early people called Canyon de Chelly home and connected their lives to the land. They used the landscape in a variety of ways. The land provided shelter, food, and other resources for survival. These first residents built no permanent homes like those evidenced in the cliff dwellings seen today. Rather, they lived in seasonal campsites. Archaeologists refer to these early people as "Basketmakers," describing a group of cultural occupation that excelled in the art of basket weaving.

*A*rchitecture of the early
Basketmaker pit house at Mummy Cave
in Canyon del Muerto. Pit houses are
usually large shallow pits up to 25 feet in
diameter and lined with large upright rock
slabs. The roof is constructed with a
meshwork of pole beams and reeds and
daubed with a thick layer of mud mortar.
Also associated with Basketmakers are
various types of cists which are usually
found in alcoves. They generally served
for grain storage or as burial tombs.

Social changes brought about new technological ideas and a change in the way of life. Subsistence relied more upon agriculture, but the people still continued to hunt and gather wild plants. Corn, beans, and squash were some of the major crops cultivated. One important technological change was the manufacturing and use of pottery. There were also architectural changes, moving from ground and subterranean areas to masonry-style shelters in the high alcoves on cliff walls.

GAIL BANDINI

GAIL BANDINI

RANDI HIRSCHMANN

Stone and adobe mortar buildings constructed in the canyon wall and protected by overhangs were less subject to erosion by rain. South-facing caves were preferred to take advantage of the low-angle light of the winter sun, with the overhang producing cool shade in the summer. Handholds and toeholds carved by hand in the rock provided access up and down sheer cliff walls.

In addition to many cliff dwellings, Canyon de Chelly offers one of the best places to see images left on stones by the past people. These images created on the canyon wall obviously involved a thought process, known only to the individual with the yucca-leaf brush who created them.

The spirit of the wind whistles through the remains of crumbled walls and empty rooms. It is believed that the materials from the building must not be reused or rebuilt, but allowed to return naturally to Mother Earth. We look through the empty ruins today and wonder, what happened to the people who once flourished here? Why did they just pick up and migrate out of the canyon? Maybe these people caused significant cultural and environmental changes that resulted in their migration. The question is a reminder, and perhaps a lesson in itself.

Cliffs and alcoves provided shelter for one or two families, using the top of the alcove as a natural roof. People in Canyon de Chelly didn't develop huge housing complexes like those found in Mesa Verde and Chaco Canyon. When people from other regions later migrated to Canyon de Chelly after their areas no longer sustained them, they brought their different architectural styles with them.

Canyon de Chelly may have served as a regional location for trade routes. Through trade and migration from other areas of the Four Corners, new ideas were brought to the canyon, including various styles of masonry work.

The spirit of the wind whistles through the remains of crumbled walls and empty rooms.

After the migration of the Ancestral Puebloans from the canyon about A.D. 1300, there is evidence to suggest the Hopis utilized the canyon for a short period of time for growing corn and, according to oral Navajo history, peaches. The Hopis never reoccupied the buildings left behind by their ancestors but built brush shelters to live in during the summer. Their seasonal migrations to the canyon were basically for farming. After harvesting the crops, they migrated out of the canyon back to the mesas.

GEORGE H. HUEY

Imprints of the five-fingered people acknowledge their connection to the special place they called home. Man was part of nature, not apart from it. Perhaps these represent the hands of those who reached out in prayer to their holy ones for spiritual guidance, or they may represent hands that provided subsistence for their families.

Images of the Past

Drawings left on canyon walls can only tell us so much about the early people who made them. The interpretation of petroglyphs (pecked into the rocks) and pictographs (painted on rocks) are limited and based only upon various scientific and personal theories. Only the person who drew it knows the true meaning of the drawing. To Native people today, these images on stones are more than what is referred to as "rock art." The people who created them probably didn't view art the way we view it today. But these were probably expressions of their spiritual connection with their gods, accounts of daily activities or experiences, or comments on their complex society and how it influenced their daily lives. These images and symbols are understood by their descendants like the Hopis, but even they are very discreet about sharing the meaning and can only relate the symbols to their clan groups.

RANDI HIRSCHMANN

This rock painting of a person holding a spear offers a glimpse of the prehistoric hunting style—or maybe even of warfare. The spear was part of a throwing device referred to as the atlatl, *used primarily for hunting small game. The atlatl was later replaced with the bow and arrow, which proved more powerful and precise. Hunting and gathering eventually gave way to farming as the primary source for food. Agricultural skills improved, and a more consistent food supply developed.*

GAIL BANDINI

*T*his Navajo petroglyph portrays the hunting style used during the 1800s. The introduction of horses made hunting more successful. Hunting and gathering remained very important even as agriculture grew. Navajos acquired horses from the Spaniards in the 1600s, allowing them to become more mobile in terms of both migration and hunting.

RALPH LEE HOPKINS

A combination of pictographs by Navajos and Ancestral Puebloans. The Navajo pictograph shows wildlife in the canyon before human impact on their territories. Today, wildlife is mostly confined to the deeper part of the canyon.

FRED HIRSCHMANN

*E*arly Navajo star ceiling located on the ceiling of an alcove about 30 to 40 feet up. Navajos believe the stars hold the sky together. Early travelers often used the alcoves for shelter and marked the ceilings with stars in the belief that they would hold the rock ceiling together.

The Navajo - The Diné

The history of the Navajo varies depending on whether information is obtained from Navajo oral histories or from historical documents.

The Diné, as we call ourselves, believe that the Holy People brought us to this land known as *Tseyi*, where we are surrounded by four sacred mountains. Within these sacred mountains is the home of our people. Before arriving at Canyon de Chelly, the Diné lived in their original homeland, an area near the east sacred mountain known as Dinétah. Many Navajos today relate their origin stories to Dinétah (also known as "Old Navajoland").

According to scientific research, the Navajos are newcomers to the Southwest and relatives of today's Apaches. Studies suggest that the Navajos are Athapascan-speaking people related to Indians living to the north and west, in what is now Canada. They split off from the others to follow game until they reached the Southwest. Soon after their arrival, they learned about farming from their new neighbors along the Rio Grande, the Pueblos. The Navajo incorporated new ideas and skills like sheep herding and agriculture to enhance their own hunting and gathering lifestyle. Perhaps because of their successful farming technique, Spanish documents in the early 1600s called them *Navajo*, "of the great cultivated fields." There was much trading going on with the Pueblo and Spanish, and at this time horses, sheep, and cattle were acquired. There was also intense conflict with the Spanish, which might have led the Navajos to move steadily westward into the Canyon de Chelly area. Life was good when the Navajos first arrived. Resources were plentiful, and the canyon provided protection and peace, serving as a refuge and fortress.

The time of peace was short lived as conflict began with neighboring tribes, the Spaniards, and later the United States military. Navajos recall this as a time of hardship and survival. The Navajos were accused of raiding, but in reality it was outside forces intruding on traditional Navajo land that forced the removal of Navajos from the canyon in 1864. More than 8,000 Navajos walked a distance of 300 miles to a place the Navajos refer to as Hweldi, *"a very hard suffering place." The four years of suffering and captivity are remembered today as the "Long Walk."*

FRED HIRSCHMANN

Absent for four long years, the Navajos longed to return to their beloved canyon. Upon release and their journey home, Navajos recall the moment when they first saw one of their sacred mountains— they burst into tears and offered prayers. It was a time of great joy to return to Canyon de Chelly, the soul of Navajoland.

GAIL BANDINI

Starting over in Canyon de Chelly was not easy. The Navajos returned to hardly anything. Before their removal from the canyon, their homes, crops, and animals were all destroyed. People tried to replant the crops but their planting yielded little for a period of time. Traditional Navajo elders believed hardship and suffering were caused by disrespecting and disobeying the teachings and beliefs of traditional values and the laws of nature. As traditional ceremonies, songs, and prayers allowed them to restore harmony, the people once again began to prosper. Today our people are a unique part of the canyon, part of the beauty and the sacredness. Visitors now have the opportunity to share these experiences.

GAIL BANDINI

BRUCE HUCKO

An *excursion by hiking, horseback, or vehicle in* *the canyon with an authorized guide provides an* *opportunity that will be long remembered.* *Authorized Navajo guides share their homeland with* *visitors from all over the world. Tour Guide David Bia* shares his stories about growing up in the canyon. These stories from personal experience, family and clan histories, and written history convey cultural values and traditions which are still valid today.

RALPH LEE HOPKINS

Horses, which used to pull plows and wagons, *are now used mainly for travel and recreation. Not* *so long ago Navajo families still traveled up and* *down the canyon using horse and wagon teams.*

Overleaf: After a day full of *activities, the canyon offers an* *opportunity for peace and solitude.* *Photo by Larry Ulrich.*

*P*atterns of Navajo farms line the bottom of the canyon today. The planting of crops and orchards has declined in recent years, as Navajo families are spending less time in the canyon during the summers. There are many reasons—climate change, employment opportunities, and educational responsibilities. The dependency on a full-time job to make a living allows people to tend to their farms only on weekends or in the evenings. Whatever crops are harvested in the fall are for family use—very little is sold or traded. Although farming has declined throughout the canyon, it is still a very important part of Navajo life today.

RALPH LEE HOPKINS

JACK OLSON

Since their introduction by the Spaniards, sheep have been an integral part of Navajo life, as their possession symbolizes wealth and is vital to the Navajo rug-weaving industry. In the 1930s the federal government forced stock reduction because of the effects of overgrazing. Whereas Navajos utilize every part of the sheep, the federal government herded the animals together, shot them, and left them to rot. Because of this, many Navajos were embittered against the government. New breeds have since been introduced which produce more meat and higher quality wool. Among many families, however, sheep tending has declined and become less important economically.

Spider Rock adopted its name from the Navajo creation story about Spider Woman, a disciplinary figure for young children. It is said that Spider Woman chose the top of Spider Rock as her home. Children were told that the sun-bleached white rock at the top of Spider Rock was bones of children who did not behave. Navajo stories also attribute the legacy of Navajo rug weaving to Spider Woman, who taught the Diné ancestors the art of weaving. Many women from Canyon de Chelly are well known for their fine tapestries.

...the children lay motionless, terrified that the Spider Woman would crawl down from her perch and snatch them from their beds.

"Heading down to the sheep camp" is an expression often used by Navajos. Horses are important for quick access in and out of the canyon or to get from one rim of the canyon to the other.

Ever since the Navajos made the canyon their permanent home around A.D. 1700, residents have acknowledged the legacy of the Ancestral Puebloans. Navajos highly respect places where these past people lived. Building a structure in an area where ancient people lived is not very common, but Standing Cow ruin is one place where there is evidence of two different cultures utilizing the same site.

The beauty of the fall season is a sign of harvest time in Canyon del Muerto. Families, including children, take a weekend or two to harvest the crops and transport them out of the canyon. Corn husks are usually left behind for livestock to graze on. The irrigation ditch in this photo is used in spring and early summer to direct water into the field for crops.

An ideal way to see the canyon if you don't mind saddle sores is by horseback. Three local outfitters offer daily and overnight pack trips during the summer from different locations of the canyons.

Evening light on the canyon walls brings peace at last to the Navajo families whose demanding chores were disrupted by visitors. The quietness brings reflection and wonder of the canyon future. The beauty of the canyon and its rich cultural history continue to draw people from all over the world to see and learn from the canyon. Maintaining a balance to share and yet preserve is very important to the families at Canyon de Chelly.

JACK OLSON

TOM BEAN

People on a horseback tour at Mummy Cave ruin reflect on the past. What was life like without the distractions imposed by today's world? People must have had a lot of time to do what? The casual visitor cannot comprehend the cultural significance the canyon holds without knowing the events and experiences that give deep meaning to the canyon.

Recreation in the Canyon

As young children, the stories and beauty of the canyon had very little meaning to us. The canyon was a playground, where we ran, climbed, and had fun. The true meaning must be preserved for our children.

Water runs in the wash only during spring runoff and summer thunderstorms. Summertime use of the canyon for recreation by the local Navajo people has increased.

Visitors may not realize they are recreating in families' backyards. Increased use of the canyon—by both Navajos and non-Navajos—will create changes, threats to the canyon residents, and a loss of their sense of home.

BRUCE HUCKO

There are still times when the canyon is quiet. The tours are done for the day and children after a fun day in the water return home to rest and look forward to another day in the canyon. Canyon residents returning to their sheep camp wonder about the unknown future and changes that will impact their privacy.

DICK DIETRICH

*T*he blossom of the fruit tree hints that spring is near. Navajo elders, through oral histories, talk about the abundance of fruit trees that used to grow along the canyon floor. The military's policy of slash and burn in the 1860s reduced the canyon orchards to what little is left today.

Life With The Seasons

The cycle of seasons in the canyon is an experience of its own. Whatever the season or time of day, you become a part of the essence of the canyon. Each spring begins a new cycle of seasons for the Navajo. People begin to prepare for their migration into the canyon and prepare the corn seeds to be planted. Often, high water from spring runoff from nearby mountains will cause some delay. The daily agenda throughout summer is filled with chores as well as fun activities for the children. Fall is a time for harvesting, and then canyon residents begin their migration back to the rim. Families spend their winter on the rim of the canyon where it is easier for children to catch the bus and people who work have better access. Before people acquired any type of transportation, summer and winter were spent inside the canyon.

*S*ummer is busy and provides little time to reflect. Children are out of school and have time to spend in the canyon with their families. Many help with chores, while others are busy with fun and play. Adults cultivate the fields, cook, weave, and even take a leisure moment under a cool shaded tree. Visitation increases, bringing hikers to explore by foot, while others enjoy seeing the canyon on horseback. For those who would rather not walk or ride a horse, motorized tours are an option.

Each spring begins a new cycle of seasons for the Navajo

FRED HIRSCHMANN

Photographs of Canyon de Chelly draw people from all over the world. As canyon residents migrate to the canyon rim, autumn draws photographers and artists to capture the color and beauty. The bright cottonwood leaves that make the canyon glow in contrast with the reddish rock wall, create a beautiful portrait evoking the peacefulness of the canyon.

GEORGE H. HUEY

Winter offers the silence and peacefulness of the rocks. Families have migrated to the rim of the canyon, leaving their summer home behind. It is time for winter stories to be shared in the warmth of the hogan—the traditional Navajo home. Creation stories are shared only in the wintertime, when the insects and animals have gone into hibernation.

GAIL BANDINI

Flowers and Spirits

The plant community of Canyon de Chelly has been an important resource for people and other creatures such as animals, insects, and birds. All the plants are known and respected to have spirit and are interconnected with other living things. The Holy People created *Nani'se,* "the growing ones." In the beginning, Mother Earth was gifted with plants to secure and stabilize the soil. All plants share the sacred gifts of air, water, light, and soil. Many plants from the canyon provide a food source, medicine for healing, and shelter. The people of the canyon learned and grew familiar with the resources offered by the canyon and used it to their advantage. To supplement their diet of mutton and corn, the canyon supplied them with piñon nuts, cactus pads and fruits, yucca flowers and pods. The piñon wood was used for fire and digging sticks, and mountain mahogany for tools. Medically, sagebrush cured coughs and headaches, and snakeweed, insect stings.

Certain plants have multiple uses. The root of the narrow-leaf yucca can be made into soap. Its fruit can be baked or dried for winter eating. Sheep and goats love to eat the blossoms. Leaves can be used as paintbrushes or for counters in the Navajo shoe game.

The natives of Canyon de Chelly believe the plants have sacred powers of healing. Before taking any part of a plant, such as this cholla cactus, a sincere prayer and a song are offered for the use of the plant.

CAROL POLICH

Free-spirited Navajo ponies race the canyon floor. Horses, sheep, and cattle are often seen, while small game such as squirrels, rabbits, skunks, and coyotes, are rarely seen. Bigger game like deer and bears are confined more to the upper region of the canyon. Tire tracks are omens of what the future holds.

The piñon tree grows at the 6,000-foot elevation and can be seen on both rim drives of the canyon. Native people have gathered piñon nuts for centuries.

BRUCE HUCKO

Chauncey Naboyia served as a guide from 1931 until his retirement in 1997. He worked with a wide range of people throughout his career including archaeologists, photographers, and many environmental groups.

TOM BEAN

Following footsteps of the past, people still make their way in and out of the canyon. Before horses and vehicles, people traveled by foot and made their way down and up these hand and footholds.

Raymond Yellowman explains the significance of the fruit tree. Raymond is a member of the Canyon de Chelly Guide Association, as are most authorized guides. The association works in conjunction with the National Park Service, and each guide is required to complete a certification process including training before being authorized.

Exploring the Canyon

Touring Canyon de Chelly with a Navajo—whether guide, ranger, or perhaps a canyon resident—lets you see the canyon through the eyes of a Native. There are several ways to see the canyon—by hiking, horseback, or motorized tours. Authorized Navajo guides who grew up in or near the canyon lead all of these tours. They provide insight into canyon history as well as their own personal experiences of growing up in the canyon. By horseback or hiking, you have the opportunity to experience the peace and quietness of the canyon. If you have very little time, don't mind the noise, and want to see as much of the canyon as possible, then a motorized tour—whether in your own four-wheel-drive vehicle or a rented one—might be for you. However you choose to visit the inner canyon, a permit and an authorized guide are required, with the exception of the White House trail.

WILSON HUNTER JR.

Rangers provide a better understanding of the people's history and their connection to the land. Navajo Park Ranger Marilyn James is fluent in the Navajo language. Navajo rangers face an added challenge absent for non-Navajos—speaking about personal feelings can sometimes feel inappropriate and be seen as giving up a part of themselves.

BRUCE HUCKO

One of the biggest challenges for many Navajo guides is cross-cultural communication. It is Common for guides to talk about people of the past and of a different culture. Sally Tsosie, a Navajo, shares her perspective of the Standing Cow ruin site and its significance to two different cultures. She has five children who were guides long before she became interested in becoming a guide herself.

"I will walk in the corn pollen path of life"

RALPH LEE HOPKINS

It is believed that corn was given to our people by the Holy Ones as a gift of life. The Navajo saying "I will walk in the corn pollen path of life" reflects the fact that corn is representative of the development of the mind, body, heart, and soul.

FRED HIRSCHMANN

Traditional chores such as wood hauling, water hauling, and caring for family, home, and livestock continue to be very important. Navajo women tend sheep to prevent them from wandering away and to protect them from predators. In the summer when children are out of school, they help with watching the sheep.

Tradition In Transition

The Navajo people of today are children of the infamous Navajo Long Walk. In the past as well as today, the Navajo confronted situations that conflicted with and challenged Navajo culture. Surviving from a near extinction, the Navajo proved ourselves both resilient and accepting of change. The Navajo thrive on new challenges and experiences, living a bicultural lifestyle which is evident by modern homes and hogans, dual languages, and traditional and contemporary dress. Many Navajos hold traditional cultural values while utilizing modern conveniences to accommodate their unique lifestyle. In Diné philosophy, for the health of our people, it is important to maintain traditions while adapting to changes in the physical world. Adherence to this belief has made the Navajo a truly bicultural society.

As Navajo people continue to survive and thrive within the canyon walls, inextricably linking their culture with the canyon landscape, Tseyi remains the epicenter of cultural renewal. The elders especially still have close ties to the land. Their stewardship and concern for the future of canyon life is inseparable from their daily activities. This is their home, their work. We have to remember as we invite outside people to the canyon, that this important "resource" is people, human beings who have a right to the respect of others, and to their privacy.

BRUCE HUCKO

Young Navajo artist Victoria Begay expresses the contrast of culture through her artwork. Many young Navajos feel that the true path lies in a melding of traditions. By listening to both voices, we may enable ourselves to speak with one.

SUGGESTED READING AND VIDEOS

GRANT, CAMPBELL. *Canyon de Chelly: Its People and Rock Art.* Tucson: University of Arizona Press, 1978.

LISTER, ROBERT and FLORENCE. *Those Who Came Before.* Tucson, Arizona: Southwest Parks and Monuments Association, 1993.

Navajo Stories of the Long Walk Period. Tsaile, Arizona: Navajo Community College Press, 1973.

REID, JEFFERSON, and STEPHANIE WHITTLESEY. *Archaeology of Ancient Arizona.* Tucson: University of Arizona, 1997.

SUPPLEE, CHARLES, and DOUGLAS and BARBARA ANDERSON. *Canyon de Chelly: The Story Behind the Scenery.* Las Vegas, Nevada: KC Publications, 1990 (revised).

The Navajo Treaty—1868. Las Vegas, Nevada: KC Publications, 1968.

THYBONY, SCOTT. *Canyon de Chelly National Monument.* Tucson, Arizona: Southwest Parks and Monuments Association, 1997.

Canyon Voices. Harper's Ferry, West Virginia: Harper's Ferry Historical Association, 1992.

Navajo Code Talkers: The Epic Story. Tully Entertainment, 1994.

All About Canyon de Chelly National Monument

Western National Parks Association

Western National Parks Association (WNPA) is a non-profit organization established to promote educational and scientific activities of the National Park Service. WNPA operates bookstores, supports interpretive programs, and provides publications for sale or free distribution at over 50 parks, including Canyon de Chelly. All net proceeds are returned to the park for projects such as producing books about Native culture, hiring volunteers for interpretive activities, conducting archaeological surveys, and rehabilitation of the park's amphitheater. WNPA provides resource material for many local schools.

For more information, contact us at:
Western National Parks Association
PO Box 588
Chinle, AZ 86503
or visit: www.wnpa.org

Prickly pear cactus
PHOTO BY GAIL BANDINI

HOW TO CONTACT US:

Call us at:
928-674-5500

Write to us at:
Canyon de Chelly NM
P.O. Box 588
Chinle, AZ 86503-0588

Visit our web site at:
www.nps.gov/cach

*Canyon de Chelly is on daylight savings time.

CANYON DE CHELLY

Junior Ranger

Become a Junior Ranger at Canyon de Chelly National Monument and...

Discover...

- *The world around you as you travel throughout the monument.*
- *Who made their home here five thousand years ago?*
- *Who lives here now?*
- *Can you read the petroglyphs – what stories do they tell you?*
- *What plants and animals live in the canyons?*
- *Hike to the White House and see the marvels that it has.*

Pick up a Junior Ranger package from the visitors center and start you journey discovering Canyon de Chelly and how important it is to preserve and take care of it. Once you have completed the assignments within the package, go see a ranger and be sworn in as an honorary Junior Ranger. *Remember - People live here, do not disturb them.*

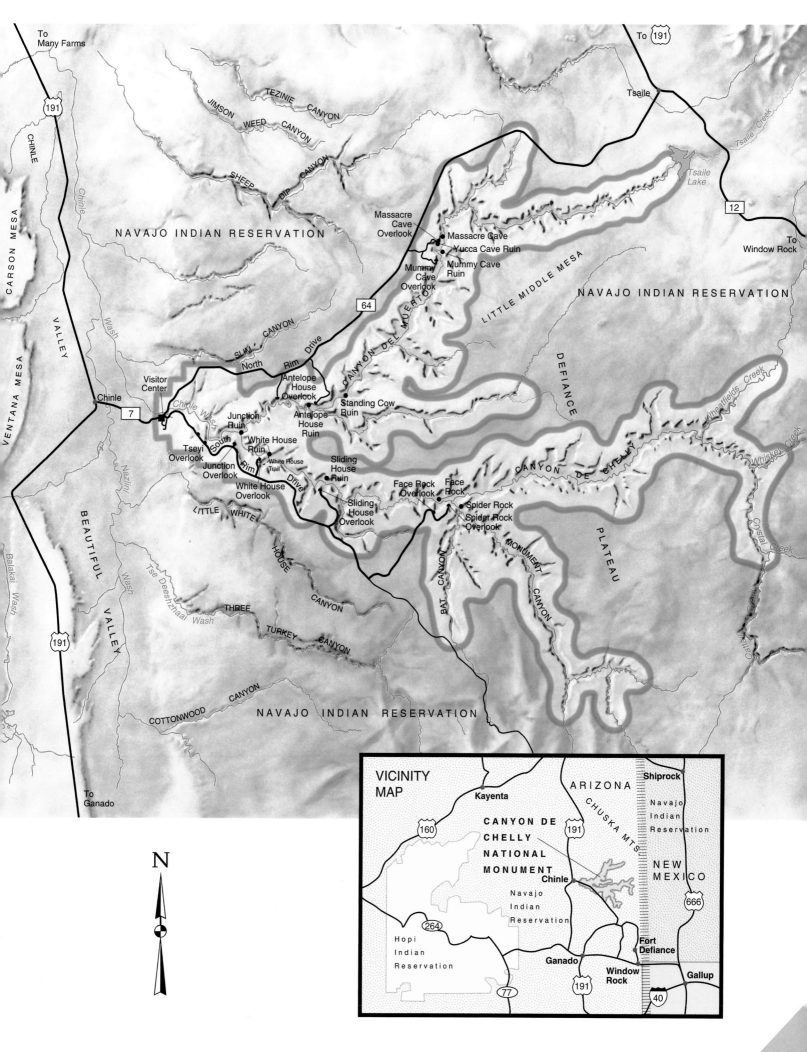

To Many Farms

CHINLE

CARSON MESA

VENTANA MESA

191

CHINLE VALLEY

Wash

Nazlini Wash

Balakai Wash

BEAUTIFUL VALLEY

191

To Ganado

JIMSON WEED CANYON

TEZINIE CANYON

SHEEP DIP CANYON

NAVAJO INDIAN RESERVATION

Chinle Wash

SLIM CANYON

North Rim Drive

64

Visitor Center

Chinle

7

Junction Ruin

Tseyi Overlook

South Rim Drive

Junction Overlook

White House Ruin

White House Trail

White House Overlook

LITTLE WHITE HOUSE CANYON

Tse Deeshzhaal Wash

THREE CANYON

TURKEY CANYON

COTTONWOOD CANYON

Antelope House Overlook

Antelope House Ruin

Standing Cow Ruin

Sliding House Ruin

Sliding House Overlook

Massacre Cave Overlook

Massacre Cave

Yucca Cave Ruin

Mummy Cave Overlook

Mummy Cave Ruin

CANYON DEL MUERTO

LITTLE MIDDLE MESA

NAVAJO INDIAN RESERVATION

DEFIANCE

Wheatfields Creek

Whiskey Creek

CANYON DE CHELLY

PLATEAU

Crystal Creek

Face Rock Overlook

Face Rock

Spider Rock

Spider Rock Overlook

BAT CANYON

MONUMENT CANYON

NAVAJO INDIAN RESERVATION

To 191

Tsaile

Tsaile Creek

Tsaile Lake

12

To Window Rock

N

45

GAIL BANDINI

Canyon de Chelly National Monument has great cultural significance to the Navajo people and other Indian tribes. Because of scientific interest in the cultural resources by research parties that frequented the canyon, and the Navajo's concern for the protection and collecting of archaeological remains, Canyon de Chelly was included in the national park system. About 130 square miles within the Navajo Reservation was set aside as a national monument on April 1, 1931. Cooperatively, the Navajo Nation and the National Park Service help visitors and Navajo people better understand the multiple cultural, historical, scientific, and natural values of Canyon de Chelly.

The canyon provides an unparalleled example of a cultural landscape reflecting the interaction and connectedness through time between the people and the land.

Welcome to the land of the Navajo which has been designated as a park known as Canyon de Chelly National Monument

TOM DANIELSEN

Canyon de Chelly provides a window of opportunity to learn about our indigenous people, their cultures and history, and having the creativity to make the human spirit really work.

KC Publications has been the leading publisher of colorful, interpretive books about National Park areas, public lands, Indian lands, and related subjects for over 45 years. We have 5 active series—over 125 titles—with Translation Packages in up to 8 languages for over half the areas we cover. Write, call, or visit our web site for our full-color catalog.

Our series are:

The Story Behind the Scenery® – Compelling stories of over 65 National Park areas and similar Public Land areas. Some with Translation Packages.

in pictures... Nature's Continuing Story® – A companion, pictorially oriented, series on America's National Parks. All titles have Translation Packages.

For Young Adventurers® – Dedicated to young seekers and keepers of all things wild and sacred. Explore America's Heritage from A to Z.

Voyage of Discovery® – Exploration of the expansion of the western United States.

Indian Culture and the Southwest – All about Native Americans, past and present.

To receive our full-color catalog featuring over 125 titles—Books, and other related specialty products:
Call (800) 626-9673, fax (928) 684-5189, write to the address below, or visit our web site at www.kcpublications.com

Published by KC Publications, P.O. Box 3615, Wickenburg, AZ 85358

Inside back cover: Ancient pictographs have endured to tell tales of the human history of this mysterious canyon. Photo by Fred Hirschmann.

Back cover: Fall view down canyon from Sliding House Overlook. Photo by Dick Dietrich.

Created, Designed, and Published in the U.S.A.
Printed by Tien Wah Press (Pte.) Ltd, Singapore
Pre-Press by United Graphic Pte. Ltd